Fish Community Monitoring at Pea Ridge National Military Park

2009 Report

Natural Resource Report NPS/HTLN/NRDS—2011/217

Hope R. Dodd and Janice A. Hinsey

National Park Service
Heartland I&M Network
Wilson's Creek National Battlefield
6424 W Farm Road 182
Republic, MO 65738

Samantha K. Mueller

University of Minnesota Duluth
Biology
207 SSB
1035 Kirby Drive
Duluth, MN 55812

December 2011

U.S. Department of the Interior
National Park Service
Natural Resource Stewardship and Science
Fort Collins, Colorado

The National Park Service, Natural Resource Stewardship and Science office in Fort Collins, Colorado publishes a range of reports that address natural resource topics of interest and applicability to a broad audience in the National Park Service and others in natural resource management, including scientists, conservation and environmental constituencies, and the public.

The Natural Resource Data Series is intended for the timely release of basic data sets and data summaries. Care has been taken to assure accuracy of raw data values, but a thorough analysis and interpretation of the data has not been completed. Consequently, the initial analyses of data in this report are provisional and subject to change.

All manuscripts in the series receive the appropriate level of peer review to ensure that the information is scientifically credible, technically accurate, appropriately written for the intended audience, and designed and published in a professional manner.

This report received informal peer review by subject-matter experts who were not directly involved in the collection, analysis, or reporting of the data. Data in this report were collected and analyzed using methods based on established, peer-reviewed protocols and were analyzed and interpreted within the guidelines of the protocols.

Views, statements, findings, conclusions, recommendations, and data in this report do not necessarily reflect views and policies of the National Park Service, U.S. Department of the Interior. Mention of trade names or commercial products does not constitute endorsement or recommendation for use by the U.S. Government.

This report is available from the Heartland Inventory and Monitoring website (http://science.nature.nps.gov/im/units/htln/) and the Natural Resource Publications Management website (http://www.nature.nps.gov/publications/nrpm/).

Please cite this publication as:

Dodd, H. R., J. A. Hinsey, and S. K. Mueller. 2011. Fish community monitoring at Pea Ridge National Military Park: 2009 report. Natural Resource Data Series NPS/HTLN/NRDS—2011/217. National Park Service, Fort Collins, Colorado.

NPS 409/111854, December 2011

Contents

Figures

Tables

Abstract

Pea Ridge National Military Park (PERI) is located in the Ozark Highlands Ecoregion of Arkansas where karst features (sinkholes, caves, springs, and losing reaches of stream) and interactions between groundwater and surface water are common. Agriculture, primarily hay fields, is the dominant land use surrounding the park, but urbanization may become an issue as the towns of Pea Ridge and Rogers expand their current jurisdictional boundaries. Many native fish populations in the Ozark Highlands have been adversely impacted by land use changes, including habitat loss and fragmentation, sedimentation, and reduced water quality.

In May 2009, Heartland Inventory and Monitoring Network (HTLN) of the National Park Service (NPS) began monitoring fish communities, physical habitat, and water quality of Pratt Creek at PERI. Four species of fish were collected in the creek. Although the fish community had moderate diversity resulting in an overall stream integrity rating of "fair", it is composed primarily of intolerant species that require clean gravel substrate for spawning. Overall, Pratt Creek provides good water quality and physical habitat to support a native fish community typical of a headwater Ozark stream.

Acknowledgments

Thanks to Tyler Cribbs, David Bowles, and Ryan Green for assistance with field work. We would also like to acknowledge the staff at PERI for their helpful advice and support.

Introduction

Pea Ridge National Military Park (PERI) is located in the Ozark Highlands Ecoregion. Karst features (sinkholes, caves, springs, and losing reaches of stream) are common in this region, creating direct interactions between ground water, surface water run-off, and streamflow. The park is approximately 17.4 km^2, containing portions of three streams as well as springs and seeps. Although two of the three streams lie primarily within the park, springs that feed into these streams have a recharge area outside park boundaries. The adjacent area surrounding the park is primarily hay fields, but urbanization may become an issue as the towns of Pea Ridge and Rogers expand.

In May 2009, the Heartland Inventory and Monitoring Network (HTLN) of the National Park Service (NPS) began monitoring water quality and fish communities of Pratt Creek at Pea Ridge National Military Park (PERI). Pratt Creek originates in the eastern part of PERI (Figure 1). It flows southwest for approximately 2.3 kilometers through forest and grasslands where it exits the southern park boundary and flows another 5.1 kilometers before its confluence with Little Sugar Creek. Winton Spring Branch, a spring with continuous flow, and Lee Creek, both originating within the park, flow into Pratt Creek just outside of the park boundary. Winton Spring Branch flows out of a rock outcropping, just north of the park road, through forest for approximately 130 meters. Lee Creek originates in the center of the park and flows for approximately 3.25 km. In spite of being spring fed, Pratt and Lee creeks become losing reaches resulting in intermittent flows during the summer season.

Changes or shifts in stream habitat complexity and water quality often determine biotic communities, including fish (Lazorchak et al. 1998). Many fish species are considered intolerant of habitat alterations and poor water quality. Assessing fish community assemblages can serve as a useful tool to identify changes in water and habitat quality (Karr 1981; Robison and Buchanan 1988; Pflieger 1997; Barbour et al. 1999; Peitz 2005). Accordingly, trends in the composition and abundance of fish populations historically have been used to assess the biological integrity of streams (Karr 1981; Barbour et al. 1999; Moulton et al. 2002). Moreover, the intrinsic value of fish to the public as environmental indicators and as a recreational opportunity makes the status of fish diversity a valuable interpretive topic for the park visitor and an informative tool for protecting and conserving the aquatic resources at PERI.

Objectives of fish community monitoring at PERI are: (1) to determine the status and long term trends in fish richness, diversity, abundance, and community composition and (2) to correlate the long-term community data to overall water quality and habitat condition.

Methods

Details on methods of site selection, fish sampling, and habitat and water quality data collection not listed in this report can be found in the Protocol for Monitoring Fish Communities in Small Streams in the Heartland Inventory and Monitoring Network (Dodd et al. 2008).

Study Area and Site Selection

A reach on Pratt Creek was selected just upstream of the Winton Spring confluence and below the park road bridge (Figure 1). Reach length was defined as 20 times the mean wetted stream width (MWSW) with a minimum of 150 m, allowing inclusion of representative channel units (riffle, run, and pool habitats) located within the stream (Moulton et al., 2002). Because the stream at PERI was small and narrow, the minimum reach length of 150 m was sampled.

Fish Collection

Fish communities were sampled in May 2009. Fish were collected using a single pass with a pulsed DC backpack electrofishing unit throughout the sampling reach. During sampling, fish were collected with nets and placed in buckets containing aerated water from the stream. All fish were identified to species where practical and counted. A subsample of 30 individuals per species were measured and weighed, and any anomalies (deformities, eroded fins, lesions, tumors, and blackspot parasite) were recorded. Fish that were too small or that were difficult to identify in the field were preserved for laboratory identification. All other fish were released back into the sample reach. Details on fish collection and sample processing techniques can be found in SOP#4 of Dodd et al. (2008).

Habitat and Water Quality

Physical habitat and water quality data were collected in conjunction with fish sampling. An 11 transect method was used to collect data on general channel morphology, fish cover, and bank conditions within the entire reach. In-stream habitat (depth, velocity, substrate, *etc.*) and fish cover (presence of boulders, hydrophytes, *etc.*) were assessed at three equally spaced points per transect (see Dodd et al. (2008), SOP #5 for a list of all habitat parameters collected). Fish cover along the banks (undercut banks, overhanging terrestrial vegetation, *etc.*) and bank/riparian stability were assessed on the left and right banks at each transect. Hourly water quality data (temperature, dissolved oxygen, pH, specific conductance, and turbidity) were collected using a calibrated water quality datalogger deployed upstream of the reach for 48 hours. Detailed methods on habitat and water quality collection are located in Dodd et al. (2008).

Data Analysis

Biological metrics that reflect fish community diversity (species richness and Simpson's Diversity Index), abundance (catch per unit effort), composition (number and percent composition of sensitive taxa), and overall stream integrity (Index of Biotic Integrity) were calculated. Community diversity was assessed using Simpson's Diversity Index, which gives the probability that two individuals picked at random from the site are the same species. Therefore, the index decreases with increasing diversity and ranges from 0 (completely diverse) to 1 (no diversity). For community composition, number and percent composition of sucker (Catastomidae), sunfish (Centrarchidae), and darter/sculpin/madtom (*Etheostoma* and *Percina*/*Cottus*/*Noturus*) species were calculated because these metrics are typically used in several Index of Biotic Integrity (IBI) calculations (Karr 1981, Dauwalter et al. 2003, Smogor

3

2005) and demonstrate sensitivity to human disturbance. The IBI developed by Dauwalter et al. (2003) was used to assess overall stream health and is calculated using seven metrics: 1) percent of individuals as algivorous/herbivorous, invertivorous, and piscivorous; 2) percent with an anomaly (disease, eroded fins, lesions, or tumors) or blackspot parasite; 3) percent as Green sunfish (*Lepomis cyanellus*), Bluegill (*Lepomis macrochirus*), Yellow bullhead (*Ameiurus natalis*), or Channel catfish (*Ictalurus punctatus*); 4) percent invertivores; 5) percent top carnivores; 6) number of darter/sculpin/madtom species; 7) number of lithophilic (sand/gravel) spawning species. Each of the seven raw metric values was scored from 0 to 10 based on upper and lower thresholds developed for the Ozarks region. The metric scores were added to calculate an IBI score that ranges from 0 to 100. Based on this IBI score, the overall integrity of the stream is classified from very poor to excellent: very poor = 0-20; poor = 20-40; fair = 40-60; good = 60-80; excellent (reference condition) = 80-100. More detailed methods on calculating biological metrics used in this report can be found in Dauwalter et al. (2003).

Physical habitat and water quality data were summarized using averages with standard errors (SE) or percentages, where appropriate. Physical habitat data were analyzed as in-stream habitat, fish cover, and bank stability. Analysis of in-stream substrate data used the Wentworth code for particle sizes (see SOP #5 in Dodd et al. 2008 for the code categories and size ranges). For assessment of stream banks, categories of bank angle, percent vegetation, height, and substrate were used to assess overall bank stability. Water quality data were summarized using means and standard errors.

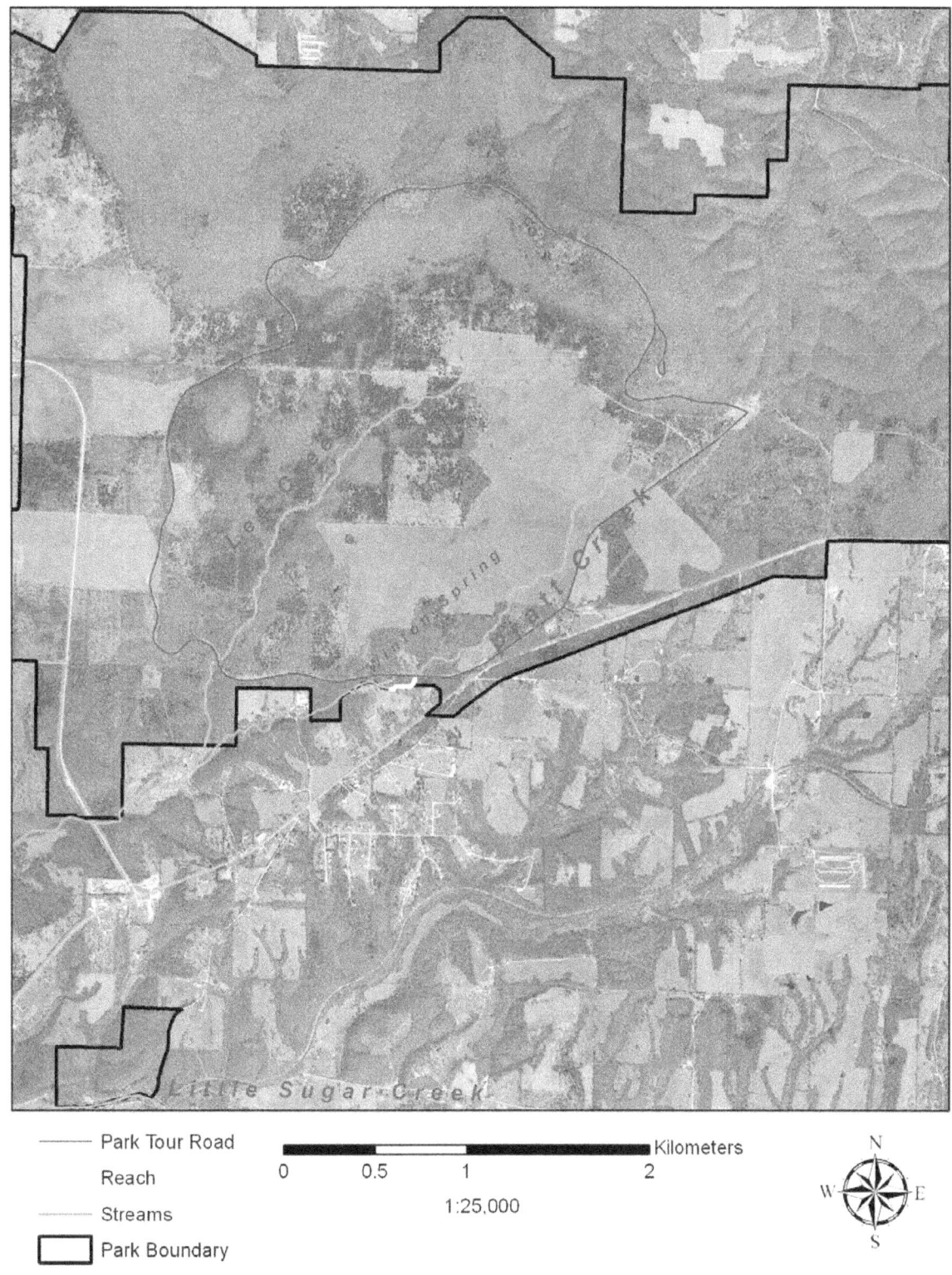

Figure 1. Reach location (yellow) in Pratt Creek for long-term fish monitoring at PERI.

Results

Fish Community

Four species were collected from Pratt Creek in 2009 (Tables 1 and 2). Three are intolerant to human disturbance (Table 2), and two are benthic species (darter and sculpin) that need clean gravel/cobble substrate. The most abundant species was the Southern redbelly dace (*Phoxinus erythrogaster*, 76.1%) and the least abundant was the Orangethroat darter (*Etheostoma spectabile*, 1.3%). No large-bodied sucker or sunfish species were collected (Table 1). The Simpson's Diversity index indicated moderate diversity (0.62) (Table 1), and stream integrity was rated as fair (IBI score of 53), due to the low number of species collected, the low percent of invertivorous fishes, and the absence of larger carnivorous fishes (Table 3).

Habitat and Water Quality

Pratt Creek was narrow (< 5m) and shallow (<30 cm) with a discharge of 0.02 m^3/s, which is typical of small headwater streams (Table 4). Dominant substrate size was large cobble (Wentworth size of 19). Fish cover was primarily small woody debris (46% of the cover) with trees/roots being the next dominant fish cover at 27%. No one fish cover type dominated more than 50% of the reach.

Banks were relatively stable. Over 59% of bank angles were less than 60° and over 90% of the banks were covered with at least 50% vegetation and were less than 2 meters in height (Table 5). Dominant bank substrates were 45.5% gravel and sand and 22.7% silt.

All water quality parameters measured in Pratt Creek, with the exception of turbidity, were within the Arkansas Pollution Control and Ecology Commission water quality standards for Ozark Highlands' surface waters (APCEC 2010) (Table 6). Average turbidity was below the APCEC standard; however, the standard was exceeded (maximum turbidity of 76 NTU) during the 48 hour logging period due to the occurrence of a storm event.

Table 1. Number of species, diversity, and percent composition of sucker, sunfish, and sculpin/madtom/darter species for Pratt Creek, 2009.

Fish Parameter	Metric Value
Species Richness	4
Simpson's Diversity	0.62
Catch Per Unit of Effort (catch/min)	15.1
Number of Sucker Species	0
% Composition of Suckers	0
Number of Sunfish Species	0
% Composition of Sunfish	0
Number of Darter, Sculpin, Madtom Species	2
% Composition of Darters, Sculpins, Madtoms	21.8

Table 2. Number of fish caught in Pratt Creek, 2009.

Family	Common Name	Scientific Name	Number Caught
Cottidae	Banded sculpin *	*Cottus carolinae*	77
Cyprinidae	Southern redbelly dace *	*Phoxinus erythrogaster*	287
Cyprinidae	Redspot chub*	*Nocomis asper*	8
Percidae	Orangethroat darter	*Etheostoma spectabile*	5

* Species intolerant to human disturbance and poor water quality conditions

Table 3. Index of Biotic Integrity (IBI) scores and metric values for Pratt Creek, 2009.

IBI Metrics	Metric Value
% Algivores, Herbivores, Invertivores, and Piscivores	0.0
% With an Anomaly (disease, eroded fins, lesions, tumors, or blackspot)	0.0
% Green sunfish, Bluegill, Yellow bullhead, or Channel catfish	0.0
% Invertivores	1.3
% Carnivores	0.0
Number of Darter, Sculpin, or Madtom Species	2
Number of Lithophilic Species (sand/gravel spawners)	4
IBI Score	53
IBI Rating	Fair

Table 4. Mean width, depth, velocity, and substrate (± one standard error) and total discharge for Pratt Creek, 2009.

Habitat Parameters	Mean	±	SE
Average Width (m)	2.9	±	0.10
Average Depth (cm)	12.6	±	1.30
Average Velocity (m/s)	0.15	±	0.02
Average Substrate (Wentworth Code)	19.3	±	0.99
Discharge (m^3/s)	0.02		

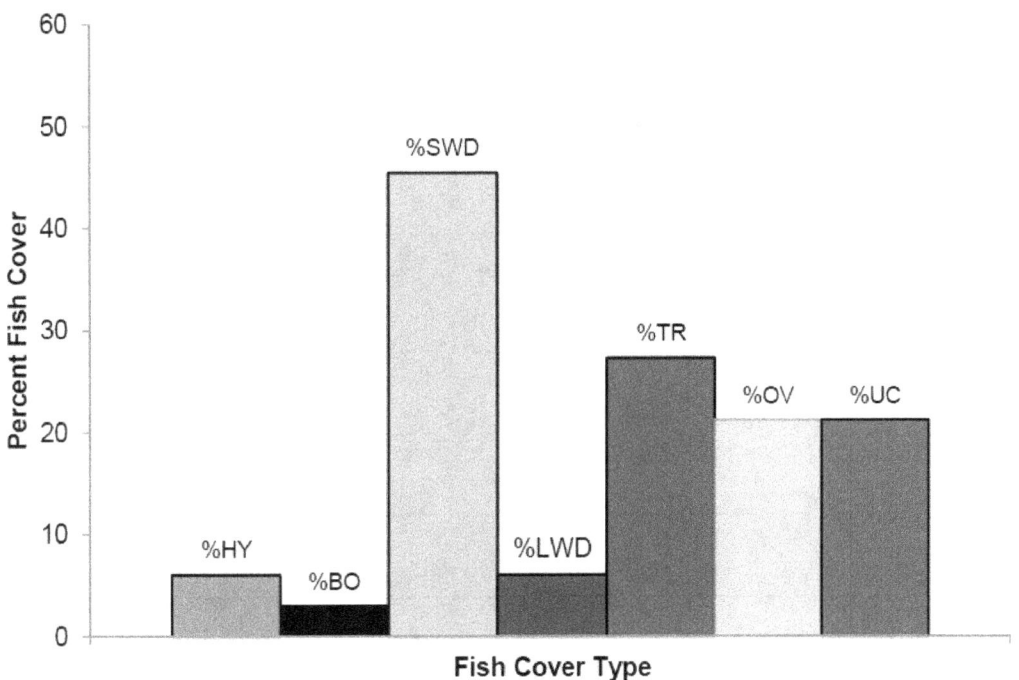

Figure 2. Percent fish cover for Pratt Creek, 2009. HY = hydrophytes, BO = boulder, SWD = small woody debris, LWD = large woody debris, TR = trees/roots, OV = overhanging vegetation, UC = undercut bank.

Table 5. Bank angle, percent vegetation, height, and substrate characteristics for Pratt Creek, 2009.

Bank Measurement	% of Occurrence
Angle	
< 60°	59.1
> 60°	40.9
% Vegetation	
> 80%	40.9
50 - 80%	50.0
< 50%	9.1
Height	
< 1m	27.3
1 - 2m	27.3
2 - 3m	36.4
> 3m	9.1
Substrate	
Bedrock/Artificial	4.5
Boulder/Cobble	13.6
Silt	22.7
Sand	13.6
Gravel/Sand	45.5

Table 6. Mean water quality parameters (+ one standard error) for Pratt Creek, 2009 and Arkansas Pollution Control and Ecology Commission water quality standards for Ozark Highlands' surface waters (APCEC 2010).

Water Quality Parameter	Mean ± SE			APCEC (2010) Standards
Water Temperature (°C)	13.2	±	0.00	≤ 29[1]
Specific Conductance (µS/cm)	230	±	8.50	N/A
Dissolved Oxygen (mg/L)	9.63	±	0.05	≥ 2 to 6[2]
pH	7.27	±	0.02	6.0 to 9.0[3]
Turbidity (NTU)	8.2	±	1.50	≤ 10[4]

[1] Not to exceed 29 °C

[2] In <26.0 km2 watersheds, minimum of 2 mg/L during critical season and 6 mg/L during primary season.

[3] Not to fluctuate > 1.0 pH unit over 24 hour period and not be < 6.0 or > 9.0.

[4] Not to exceed 10.0 ntu during base flows.

Discussion

Although the fish community of Pratt Creek had low species richness, moderate diversity, and a stream integrity rating of fair, the community was composed of predominately intolerant species in high abundance and had low occurrence of disease and anomalies. In addition, water quality was good in Pratt Creek and well within state standards. The low fish diversity and stream integrity rating is likely due to Pratt Creek being an intermittent stream above Winton Spring, having low water levels and only moderate amounts of fish cover available to support high numbers of species, particularly larger-bodied species. In September 2003, Justus and Petersen (2005) collected three species in Pratt Creek. Both the Southern redbelly dace (most abundant species) and Banded sculpin (*Cottus carolinae*) were found in the creek during their inventory. The Redspot chub (*Nocomis asper*), however, another sensitive species found in our collections, was absent from the 2003 survey. Ground water influence from Winton Spring may act as a refuge, providing adequate water to sustain these sensitive species downstream during drought years, allowing them to recover during wetter years. In summary, Pratt Creek provides good water quality and physical habitat in support of a native fish community typical of small Ozark Highland streams.

Literature Cited

Arkansas Pollution Control and Ecology Commission (APCEC). 2010. Regulation No. 2, As Amended Regulation Establishing Water Quality Standard for Surface Waters of the State of Arkansas. Arkansas Pollution Control and Ecology Commission Report. Arkansas Pollution Control and Ecology Commission, Little Rock, Arkansas.

Barbour, M. T., J. Gerritsen, B. D. Snyder, and J. B. Stribling. 1999. Rapid bioassessment protocols for use in streams and wadeable rivers: periphyton, benthic macroinvertebrate, and fish, 2nd edition. EPA 841-B-99-002, U.S. Environmental Protection Agency, Washington, DC.

Dauwalter, D. C., E. J. Pert, and W. E. Keith. 2003. An index of biotic integrity for fish assemblages in Ozark Highland Streams of Arkansas. *Southeastern Naturalist* 2:447-468.

Dodd, H. R., D. G. Peitz, G. A. Rowell, D. E. Bowles, and L. M. Morrison. 2008. Protocol for monitoring fish communities in small streams in the Heartland Inventory and Monitoring Network. Natural Resource Report NPS/HTLN/NRR—2008/052. National Park Service, Fort Collins, Colorado.

Karr J. R. 1981. Assessment of biotic integrity using fish communities. *Fisheries* 6:21–27.

Lazorchak, J. M., Klemm, D. J., and D. V. Peck. 1998. Environmental monitoring and assessment program-surface waters: field operations and methods for measuring the ecological condition of wadeable streams. EPA/620/R-94/004F. U.S. Environmental Protection Agency, Washington, DC.

Moulton, S. R. III, J. G. Kennen, R. M. Goldstein, and J. A. Hambrook. 2002. Revised protocols for sampling algal, invertebrate, and fish communities as part of the National Water-Quality Assessment Program. U.S. Geological Survey, Reston, Virginia. Open-file Report 02-150.

Peitz, D.G. 2005. Fish community monitoring in prairie park streams with emphasis on Topeka shiner (*Notropis Topeka*): summary report 2001-2004. National Park Service, Fort Collins, Colorado.

Pflieger, W. L. 1997. The fishes of Missouri. Missouri Department of Conservation, Jefferson City, Missouri.

Robison, H. W., and T. M. Buchanan. 1988. Fishes of Arkansas. University of Arkansas Press, Fayetteville, AR.

Smogor, R. 2005. Draft manual for interpreting Illinois fish IBI scores. Illinois Environmental Protection Agency, Bureau of Water, Surface Water Section.